I0108456

# Dino the ~~Dinosaur~~ Dog

All Rights Reserved.
Copyright © 2018 Written by RT Slayton.
Copyright © 2018 Illustrated by Sofia Rayas

RT Publishing

Printed in the United States of America

All rights reserved. No part of this book may be used or reproduced in any manner whatsoever without written permission except in the case of a brief quotation embodied in critical articles and reviews. For information address RT Publishing.

Cover and Illustrations by Sofia Rayas

# Dino

# the

# ~~Dinosaur~~

# Dog

Authored by RT Slayton

Illustrated by Sofia Rayas

Hello, my name is Bobby and this is my best friend — Dino.

My family and I got Dino when he was just a puppy. Like me, Dino had lots of brothers and sisters. With all those puppies we thought it would be hard choosing which dog would be ours.

But while all the other puppies played and wrestled with each other, one cute, little, brown and white fur ball chose us to be his family.

We named him after a cartoon character from The Flintstones. Sitting at dinner one night trying to decide on a name...

...my dad said, "How about Fred?" My mom said "How about Barney?"...

Then all the kids yelled "DINO"!

Dino loved to run through our neighborhood with me chasing after him. Sometimes I would catch him...

...most times not.

It was a good thing that one of my friend's dad was the Chief of Police because we got to know the policemen in our town very well. Dino loved to adventure through our side of town. Sometimes the policemen would find him and give him a ride in their police car.

Dino loved to sit in the back seat with his head out the window.

"Bobby - please try to keep Dino on his leash." The officers would say to me when they brought him back home.

Penny was Dino's girlfriend. They loved to chase each other around her back yard and play tug-of-war with a braided rope toy.

Dino loved adventure. Once he climbed out onto the roof of our house with my brother and me.  We thought it was fun but my older sister was not at all happy with us.

On hot summer days we would go down to the river to cool off and swim. Dino loved to run off the dock and leap as far as he could into the water.

When our family moved out into the country, just outside of town, Dino would still visit our old neighborhood. If he got tired, Dino would go to our old house to relax in his favorite sleeping spot.

The people who now lived in the house would find Dino sleeping in their garage and call us to come down and get him.

At our new house Dino would spend his days chasing rabbits down into holes...

or squirrels up into trees.

Once he found out why you don't chase
Skunks — Pee Yew!

Dino is not a young dog anymore, so we like to spend our time sitting on the deck of the house relaxing in the sun and looking out over our town.

Best friends
forever.

# About the Author

RT Slayton is a lifelong owner and lover of dogs. After emerging from the 9-5 routine he has found his passion for writing about dogs as well as painting portraits of family pets. He also volunteers as a "dog walker" for an organization that trains dogs to assist people with physical disabilities.

RT also wants to share his fond memories, and the experiences he had owning dogs with other dog lovers.

# About the Illustrator

The illustrator, Sofia Rayas, is a high school senior and aspiring animator. She has been drawing since she was little and is excited to continue creating art for stories in college. She has owned two lovely black labs and hopes to share the love of wild and happy dogs with everyone.

www.ingramcontent.com/pod-product-compliance
Lightning Source LLC
Chambersburg PA
CBHW041552040426

42447CB00002B/146